THIS WALKER BOOK BELONGS TO:

_____

_____

_____

_____

Common European Hamster
(Very aggressive)

Dwarf

Grey

Satin Coated
(Coat is not waterproof)

Albino

Banded

To Sara

With thanks to John Barker, B. Vet. Med., M.R.C.V.S.

First published 1995 by
Walker Books Ltd, 87 Vauxhall Walk
London SE11 5HJ

This edition published 1996

2 4 6 8 10 9 7 5 3

This book has been typeset in Monotype Garamond.

Printed in Hong Kong

British Library Cataloguing in Publication Data
A catalogue record for this book is
available from the British Library.

ISBN 0-7445-4379-7

How to Look After Your
HAMSTER

Colin and Jacqui Hawkins

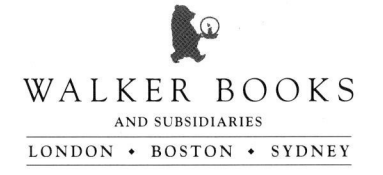

WALKER BOOKS

AND SUBSIDIARIES

LONDON • BOSTON • SYDNEY

Hamster Facts

Did you know "hamster" comes from the German word "*hamstern*" meaning hoarder? This is because hamsters store food in pouches in their cheeks.

This should keep me going until lunch-time.

There are many varieties of hamster, and they come in different colours, coat-types and sizes.

Salaam!

You got here just in time. We were nearly extinct.

Golden hamsters are the most popular type. They are all descended from a single female and her family found in Syria in 1930. Because they are desert animals, hamsters sleep during the day (when it is hot) and wake up in the evening.

The Common or European hamster can be very aggressive and may spit when angry.

The Rex Coated hamster has curly fur and even curly whiskers.

The Albino hamster is completely white with pink eyes.

Most hamsters will fight when they are put together. Only the dwarf Russian hamster prefers company.

How to Choose a Hamster

Hamsters live for about two years, so choose a young one aged between five and eight weeks. Both males and females make good pets, but make sure that a female has always lived in an all-female cage – otherwise she might be expecting babies!

What to look for

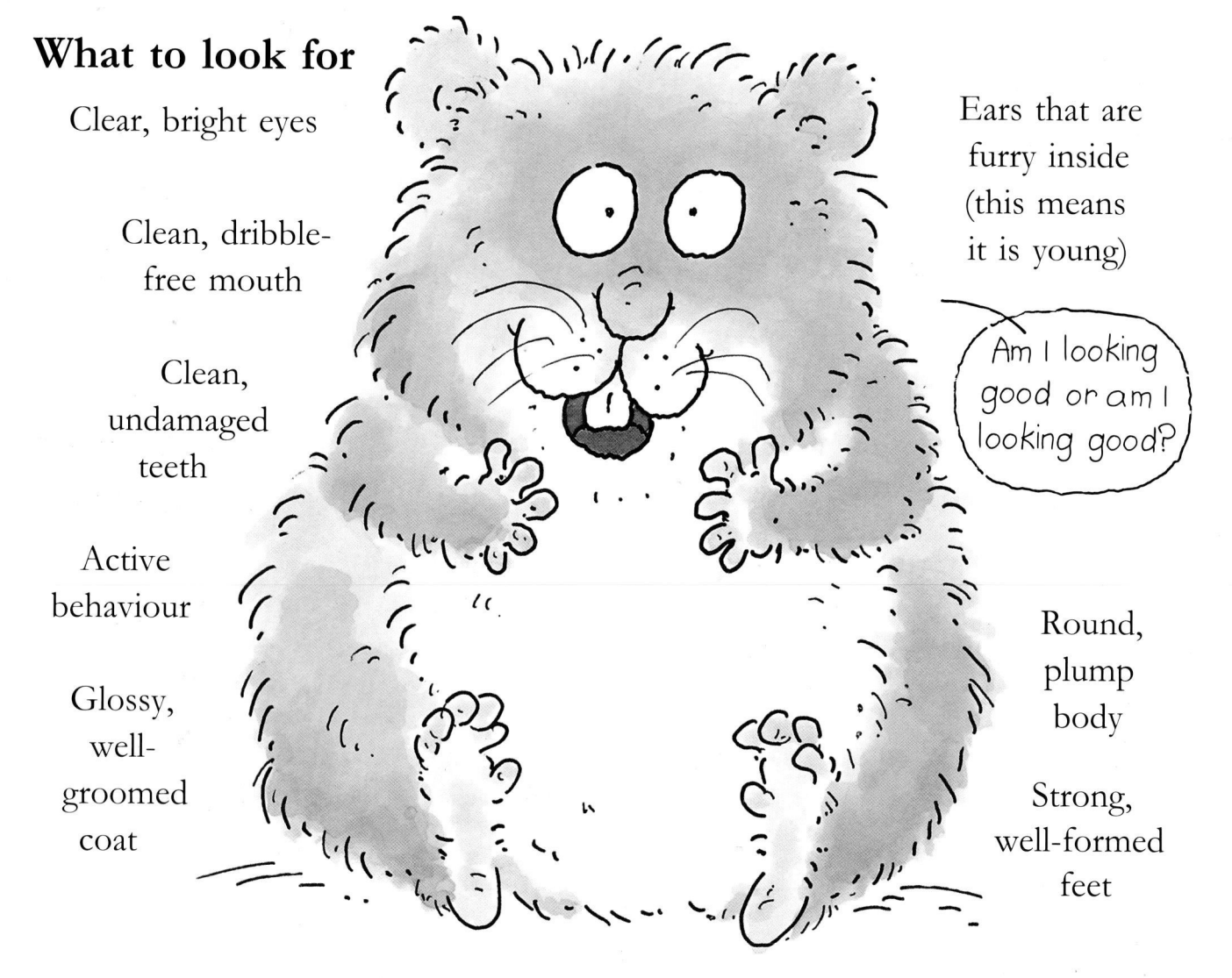

Clear, bright eyes

Clean, dribble-free mouth

Clean, undamaged teeth

Active behaviour

Glossy, well-groomed coat

Ears that are furry inside (this means it is young)

Am I looking good or am I looking good?

Round, plump body

Strong, well-formed feet

Do not choose…

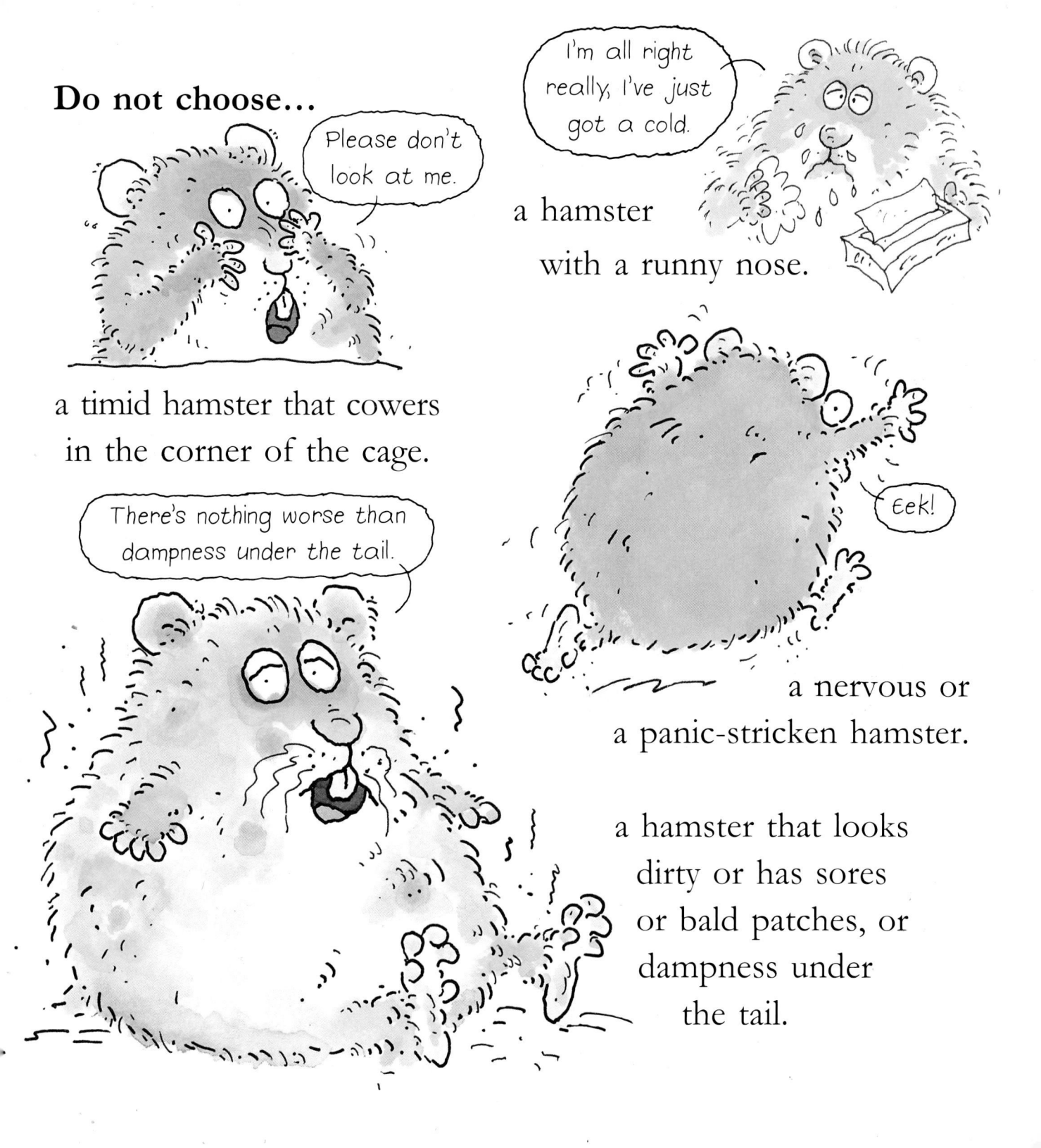

Please don't look at me.

a timid hamster that cowers in the corner of the cage.

I'm all right really, I've just got a cold.

a hamster with a runny nose.

Eek!

a nervous or a panic-stricken hamster.

There's nothing worse than dampness under the tail.

a hamster that looks dirty or has sores or bald patches, or dampness under the tail.

Bringing Your Hamster Home

A hamster makes a good pet, but before you buy one make sure you have time to feed him, play with him and keep him clean. Bring your hamster home in a comfortable, well-ventilated box.

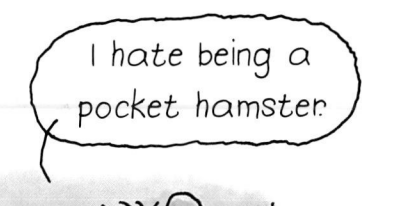

Once you have put your pet in his new home, leave him to settle down for a few hours. Hamsters are very shy, so make friends gently.

Never poke at the cage with a stick or pencil. This will make the hamster nervous.

A Hamster Home

Cages come in all shapes and sizes. Hamsters are very active and need space to run and climb, so choose a cage with plenty of room for exercise.

Circular, stacking cages are good. They don't take up much room and have several floors for the hamster to explore.

Put absorbent litter such as peat or sawdust on the floor of the cage.

Wow! What a pad!

Put the cage in a place that is always warm, but not in direct sunlight…

and well away from draughts.

Make sure there is a nesting box.

Hamsters love to burrow, so fill the box with lots of bedding material, such as hay or white shredded paper.

Your hamster needs plenty of fresh water every day. Attach a drip-fed water bottle to the side of the cage.

Every home should have one of these.

Put food in a heavy dish your hamster can't tip over.

Nnnnaa...

Yuk! I hate plastic.

Never use a plastic bowl. Your hamster will gnaw it and plastic splinters may pierce his pouches.

Keeping Your Hamster Happy

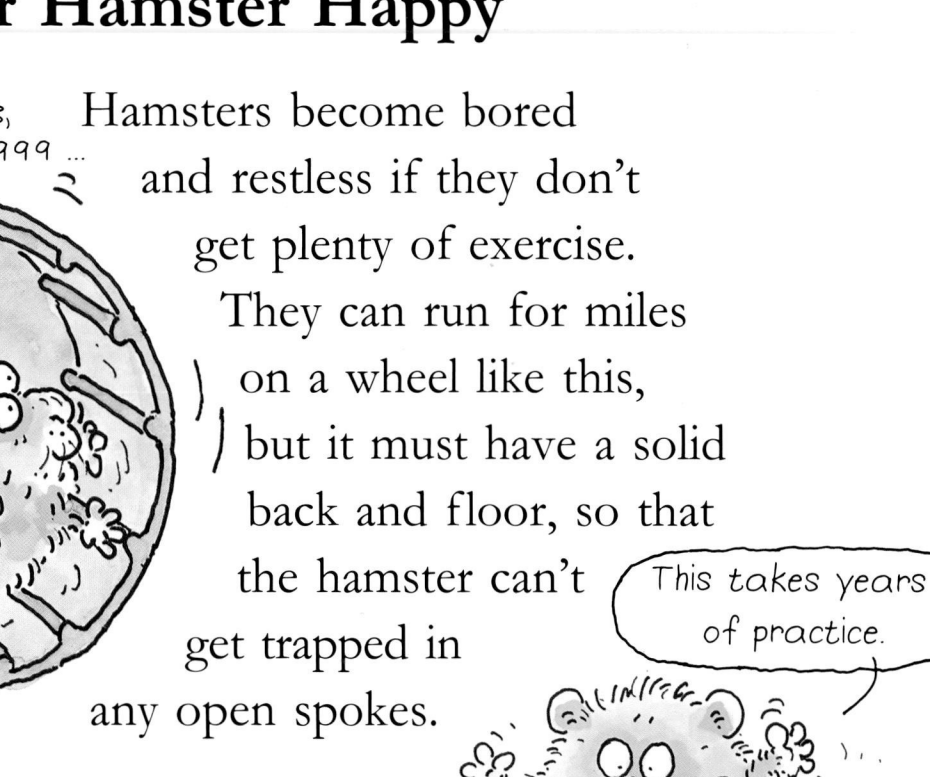

Hamsters become bored and restless if they don't get plenty of exercise. They can run for miles on a wheel like this, but it must have a solid back and floor, so that the hamster can't get trapped in any open spokes.

997, 998, 999 ...

This takes years of practice.

Wooden cotton reels are safe toys and toilet rolls can provide plenty of fun.

This is called "The Toilet Roll".

Your hamster will soon learn to enjoy a climbing frame...

and ramps are good for scrambling up and sliding down.

A jamjar is an effective and cheap toy, but make sure it is big enough for your hamster to get in and out easily.

Hamster Food

Hamsters like a varied diet. Mixed seeds, grains and nuts are their basic food and can be bought from the pet shop.

Just off to the pet shop for lunch.

They also enjoy a few porridge oats.

I really love my porridge oats.

An adult hamster needs only about 15 g (½ oz) of food once a day.

I won't need seconds.

Don't try and feed your hamster in the morning – he will be too sleepy. The best feeding time is in the evening, when he wakes up.

I'm always too tired to eat breakfast.

Hamsters love to gnaw, and this stops their teeth growing too long. Let your pet chew on a piece of raw carrot or a dog biscuit.

Hamsters should have some fresh fruit or vegetables every day, and try pieces of hard-boiled egg or flakes of cooked fish occasionally.

Never give your pet oranges, crisps, salted nuts or chocolate. These are not natural foods for hamsters and can make them very ill.

Hamster Hygiene

Help your hamster stay clean and healthy by keeping the cage in good condition.

Once a week...

Put your pet in a safe place and give the whole cage a thorough spring-clean.

Change the litter on the floor of the cage and replace the hay or paper in the nesting box. Always use plain white paper in the box – coloured inks are poisonous.

Your hamster will shred and arrange the material until he's comfortable.

Every day…

Remove any uneaten food before it goes mouldy. In particular, check the hamster's food store for bits of fruit and vegetable that might start to rot.

> A tidy home is a clean home.

> I could eat my dinner off this.

Thoroughly wash out the feeding bowl and the water bottle. Refill the bottle with fresh water.

Remove droppings. Hamsters can be trained to use a small tray as a toilet. This makes daily cleaning very easy.

> Jolly useful these trays.

Handling Your Hamster

Sorry, but I'm frightened.

It is important to learn how to handle your hamster properly or he will become bad-tempered and unfriendly.

He may be frightened and try to bite you at first, so be gentle and don't rush. Make sure he is fully awake before you start to make friends.

Hamsters are short-sighted but have a good sense of smell. Let him get to know you by offering him your fingers to sniff.

Sniff! Sniff! I know that smell.

Once you have made friends you can pick your hamster up. Place your hand gently but firmly over his back and curl your fingers gently under his stomach.

Cup your other hand underneath and scoop him up to make him feel warm and secure.

When you first pick your hamster up make sure you are close to the ground, in case he wriggles free.

Be patient and you will soon have a lovable and friendly pet.

Grooming

Hamsters are very clean animals and will spend a great deal of time washing themselves with their front paws.

They will bite on hard food like carrots and apples to keep their teeth clean and stop them growing too long.

You should visit the vet if the hamster's teeth or claws get too long.

Very dirty hamsters can be cleaned with a cotton bud dipped in warm water.

Long-haired hamsters need to be lightly brushed each day with a soft toothbrush.

Hamsters will often start to groom themselves when they are faced with a problem or a new situation.

Hamster Health

Hamsters can catch colds
or flu from humans, so if you
are unwell ask a friend to feed
your pet and clean the cage.

I don't feel well.

It's no good.
I just can't go.

Plenty of fruit and
moistened vegetables will
prevent or cure constipation.

*Always remember to
wash your hands before
and after handling your
hamster or cleaning
out the cage.*

Take your hamster to the vet if…

you think he has diarrhoea or "wet tail". This can be fatal.

When you've got to go, you've got to go.

Get me a vet, quick!

his head becomes swollen. It could mean he has an abscess in one of his pouches or that some food has got stuck there.

You should see the other guy.

he has cuts or broken bones from falling or from fighting with another hamster.

Breeding

As hamsters usually live on their own they will not get pregnant unexpectedly. If you want to breed hamsters think very carefully before you begin. It is quite a difficult business.

Hamsters can start breeding from the time they're eight weeks old. The male and female should be introduced gradually.

The female can get very aggressive if she's put with the male too quickly. Once they have mated they should be separated immediately.

A hamster's pregnancy only lasts sixteen days. She will need plenty of good food and water all through that period.

Thank goodness it's only 16 days.

The hamster mother will not need any help when she has her babies, and you should leave the family alone for a few days afterwards. The babies will be weaned at three weeks old but will start fighting at six weeks, so they will need to be put in separate cages.

Hamsters have large litters of five to seven cubs – make sure you can find them all good homes before you let your pet breed.

Five ... Six ... Seven.

Mum! *Mum!* *Mum!* *Mum!*

Hamster Hints

Never disturb a sleeping hamster. He will panic and may bite.

LET SLEEPING HAMSTERS LIE

KNOCK! KNOCK!

Who's there? If you want to coax your pet out of the nesting box, tap gently on the side of the cage and tempt him out with his favourite titbit. He will soon learn to come out when you tap.

What's in here?

Hamsters do enjoy a free run out of their cages from time to time, but they are experts at escaping. If your hamster runs away, entice him back with pieces of his favourite food in a jamjar.

Hamsters have no idea when they are up high and can injure themselves seriously if they fall. Watch your pet carefully when he's out of the cage and always handle him over a table in case you drop him.

If the temperature of the cage drops too low your hamster may go into hibernation. If that happens, warm him gently in your hands and let him wake up slowly.

You hamster will have a natural instinct to burrow, so he may enjoy having a tray or bucket of sterilized earth to dig in.

Long-haired Piebald   Golden Syrian   Golden Spotted

Chinese

(When it snows the dark stripe on this hamster's back turns white)

Smoke Pearl

MORE WALKER PAPERBACKS
For You to Enjoy

Also by Colin & Jacqui Hawkins

HOW TO LOOK AFTER YOUR...

Four brilliant pet-care books, packed with information for the young, would-be pet owner.

"A must... There are useful tips on home, feeding, health
and much more with fun drawings." *R.S.P.C.A. Animal Action*

How to Look After Your Cat   0-7445-4737-7
How to Look After Your Dog   0-7445-4738-5
How to Look After Your Hamster   0-7445-4379-7
How to Look After Your Rabbit   0-7445-4380-0
£4.99 each

COME FOR A RIDE ON THE GHOST TRAIN

"Every page must be turned with care as a comic, but wholly
scary surprise is revealed under the simplest flaps. Irresistible."
Julia Eccleshare, The Bookseller

0-7445-3671-5   £4.99

TERRIBLE TERRIBLE TIGER/THE WIZARD'S CAT

Two wonderfully entertaining rhyming picture books about a tiger
who is not quite what he seems and a cat who wishes he were something else!

Terrible Terrible Tiger   0-7445-5230-3   £4.50
The Wizard's Cat   0-7445-5231-1   £4.50

Walker Paperbacks are available from most booksellers, or by post from B.B.C.S., P.O. Box 941, Hull, North Humberside HU1 3YQ
24 hour telephone credit card line 01482 224626

To order, send: Title, author, ISBN number and price for each book ordered, your full name and address,
cheque or postal order payable to BBCS for the total amount and allow the following for postage and packing:
UK and BFPO: £1.00 for the first book, and 50p for each additional book to a maximum of £3.50.
Overseas and Eire: £2.00 for the first book, £1.00 for the second and 50p for each additional book.

Prices and availability are subject to change without notice.